MW00935437

Essentials for Frontline Living

Leslie Bishop-Joe

XULON PRESS

Essentials for Frontline Living
by Leslie Bishop-Joe

Printed in the United States of America

ISBN 978-1-60477-424-5

Unless otherwise indicated, Bible quotations are taken from the King James Version of the Bible.

www.xulonpress.com

Table of Contents

I am so very grateful to the Lord for bringing to fruition that which He placed within me over the past several years. Our God is so faithful, and He sent the greatest friend and companion that we could ever hope for in the Person of the Holy Spirit. He continues to be my Guide and greatest Encourager.

My thoughts and prayers go out to every woman in ministry, and while my hope is that this book will be a source of encouragement for anyone who is led to read it, I particularly pray for the strength and fortitude of God's women. Although there will be times of misunderstanding, isolation, and feelings of despair, just take courage in the fact that there is absolutely no failure in our God. Be encouraged to fight the good fight of faith, regardless of the circumstances.

Thanks to my family for your ongoing support. To my husband, Clarence; my sons, Charles, Rashaan, Brian, and Leon; and my dear daughters-in-law, Tammy and "Joy" (Arishandria). You are truly gifts to me.

Many thanks to Lisa Silver, who has served as my adjutant and friend. Thank you for working tirelessly on this project as though it was your own. Thanks for many long hours and late nights of reading, typing, and listening to me as I shared what I felt the Spirit was leading me to share through this book.

I dedicate this work to my precious grandchildren, Tiara, T'Nia, Tasia, Naiyel, "B.J." (Brian Jr.), and "Jazzy" (Jasmine), who mean the world to me. My sincere prayer for you is that you would become frontline warriors even in your youth.

Prepare to A.R.R.I.V.E.

God's will for each of His children is that we would fulfill our God-given destiny and arrive at the place that He has ordained for our lives before the foundation of the world. He has a plan and a purpose for our lives and has made provision for us to arrive and not to abort the plan.

A—(Appointment)

Know that God has set up divine appointments throughout the course of our lives. As the Spirit of God shows us glimpses of where the Lord is taking us and what His plan is for our lives, we must prepare accordingly in order to be ready for the appointed time.

R—(Response)

Learn the appropriate response. The only appropriate response to the King is, "Yes, Lord." Always, yes. Our attitude with the response must be "nevertheless, not my will but Thine be done."

R—(Revelation)

Here we don't speak of new revelation but that which is specific to you. God's purpose for you will be revealed to you. This cannot be validated by other men. God knows where He's taking you, and only He knows how to get you there. Let Him show the way, and He will bring into your life those who are a part of His plan and purpose to cause His will to come to fruition in your life.

I—(Instructions/Integrity)

It is not enough for us to have revelation, but we must know how to carry it out. Just because the Lord has shown you what He wants you to do does not mean that it's time to move or act on that revelation now. Wait for instructions. Always walk in integrity and refuse to compromise the instructions that God has given to you. We don't have to try to network and make things happen. When it's of God, He will bring it to pass.

V—(Vashti)

Remember the Vashti in Esther's life, and pray for the Vashtis in your life. Be aware that there is often a Vashti in the lives of those whom the Lord has called to greatness. For David, it was Saul. David had to maintain his integrity and walk in God's anointing until God's set time. Stay humble and remember that as God transitions us into a place, it's not necessarily because we are the better one; rather, it's about the change of seasons. Resist the temptation to seek power, position, or prestige when it appears that someone now occupies the place or places where the Lord has shown you that He will take you. In His timing, God will orchestrate your transition.

E—(Endurance/Expectation)

We must have our minds made up to endure. Many haven't obtained that which God has revealed to them simply because they have halted between two opinions and haven't made up their minds to believe God. Live with expectation. Trust God's favor. Know that He is faithful and that He has an expected end planned for you. Know that He has preceded you in every situation. We speak of praising Him and thanking Him in advance of our blessings or the answers to our prayers, but in reality, we can't thank or praise Him in advance because there is no way to get ahead of Him. He's already in our tomorrows.

The New Birth

Nicodemus saith unto him, How can a man be born when he is old? Can he enter the second time into his mother's womb?

—John 3:4

W e operate in the midst of two different kingdoms that coexist. The principles of these two kingdoms differ extensively; however, the way to enter each of them is through the process of birth.

Each of us was born to an earthly set of parents and became a part of this earthly kingdom, or what we as the Christian community know as the "world." We learn what we know of this world and its systems primarily from our parents or caretakers, who impart what they know of it through their upbringing, teachings, and experiences.

It's amazing how one's entrance into the Kingdom of God is likened to that of the natural birth. Newborns must be cared for and nurtured in order to develop into normal, healthy, functioning human beings capable of contributing to society in a positive manner. We can go through our entire lives living side by side with a heavenly Kingdom but never realizing it. It is veiled from us until we are birthed into it. This Kingdom is spiritual and cannot be perceived with our natural abilities.

Jesus told Nicodemus in John 3:1-8 that in order to see the Kingdom of heaven, he must be "born again." This was certainly not a reference to physical birth, since Nicodemus was by then a grown man. Jesus spoke of a spiritual process, which Nicodemus had to be willing to accept and experience by faith. This spiritual birth is just as real as the natural one that had brought Nicodemus into the world.

So then, the first principle for entering the Kingdom of God is that one must be born again. Jesus said that we must be born of the water (natural birth) and of the spirit (our spiritual rebirth) (John 3). Then just as newborn babes, we must be fed and nurtured. As babes in Christ, we are not able to feed ourselves, but must desire the sincere milk of the Word that we may grow thereby (1 Pet. 2:2).

This new birth can take place at any given time in an individual's life after he has reached an age wherein he is able to make a decision. Since there are no barriers in who may come to the Lord, everyone from young children to the elderly has an opportunity to accept Him. Babes in Christ cannot be readily identified by their age or appearance. This can be problematic, as those who are new converts often are ushered into Kingdom work based upon their natural abilities. This practice causes the church to miss a crucial step in Kingdom principles. That is the step of teaching or making disciples. It is necessary if the church is to develop strong, healthy babies into mature, functioning members of the body of Christ who are equipped to do their part in the advancing of the Kingdom of God.

Attempting to operate in God's Kingdom by earthly principles will bring utter frustration, and it will bring spiritual growth to a quick halt, a dead end. Worldly, or earthly principles are opposed to the principles of God. If we desire to grow and advance in the Kingdom of God and be used by Him, we must be willing to let worldly principles go and learn the Lord's ways. Because the two kingdoms coexist, many have been around the church setting and have learned "church culture," "church lingo," and how to act in the church environment in order to be accepted. What we fail to realize, though, is that they are babes. Some are in adult bodies and are able to do adult things, but in the Kingdom, they are babes and must be nurtured, taught, and built up in the Word of God in order to be profitable to the work of the ministry.

God's Word is meat to us, but it also serves as a part of our spiritual weaponry, for it was by knowledge and skillful use of the Word that Jesus was able to resist the devil and cause him to flee (Luke 4). For the Word is quick and powerful and sharper than any two-edged sword (Heb. 4:12). As newborn babes, we need time to become rooted and grounded in truth (2 Pet. 3:18), to learn His character and His ways so that we may become His disciples indeed. We must study to show ourselves approved unto God (*not unto men*), a workman that needeth not to be ashamed, rightly dividing the word of truth (2 Tim. 2:15). Truth that isn't rightly divided is error. Without those who are skilled in the Word to instruct us in righteousness when we are babes, we will walk in error in many areas of our Christian experience. The Word of God is given for doctrine, reproof, correction, instruction in righteousness (2 Tim. 3:16), and the gifts and ministries within the church are given for the perfecting of the saints (Eph. 4:12). These steps of laying a firm foundation are vital to the growth and development of the believer and should not be neglected.

As babes in the natural, we soon learn to get around on our own by crawling and eventually walking. As born-again believers, we too, must take responsibility for studying God's Word and eventually learning to walk by faith. Our Christian walk is not governed by what we see or perceive, or by our earthly circumstances. God has called us to a life that must be governed, or led, by our faith. For we walk by faith and not by sight (2 Cor. 5:7); for the just shall live by his faith (Heb. 2:4). There is no other way to enter or to operate in the Kingdom of God except by faith.

Not unlike our natural birth, when we are born again, we are born into a kingdom of which we have no knowledge. Many have grown up around the "church scene" for years prior to making a decision to come to Christ. All knowledge at that point is second-hand. We hear the testimonies of our parents and others, and although they may be valid and strong, they won't empower us. They will encourage us, but God's will is to give us a personal testimony. We can't stand and give someone else's testimony, for then it carries no power. We overcome by the blood of the Lamb and by the word of our testimony (Rev. 12:11). Our testimony carries so much power because no one can take it from us. No one can refute it because it's ours, and it has power because the theme of any testimony that a child of God has is that "God did it!" God has a plan, a blueprint, for each of us that is designed to ultimately bring glory to Himself.

Moment of Reflection

We must first grasp, or accept, salvation by faith, for faith is the key to our operating within the Kingdom of God.

From Transformation to Transition

I beseech you therefore, brethren, by the mercies of God, that ye present your bodies a living sacrifice, holy, acceptable unto God, which is your reasonable service.

Romans 12:1, 2

What a wonderful mystery it is to experience the power of God's Word to transform an individual from the inside out, by the renewing of a degenerate and fallen mind. The minds of thieves, murderers, whoremongers, adulterers, fornicators, and all who oppose God can be renewed, thus making way for the individual to be transformed to one who hears God and seeks to please Him. Countless lives have been transformed and then transitioned to a place where they become exceptional gifts to the body of Christ and examples of God's presence in the earth.

Romans 12:2 admonishes: "Be not conformed to this world: but be ye transformed by the renewing of your mind." Sin has plunged man into an unrighteous state that governs our thinking as well as our actions and reactions to situations. However, this is certain death to the individual believer and to the church. A carnal, unregenerate mind is enmity with God. Likewise, the mind of the believer, if not in a constant mode of renewal, will not be transformed. The mind that is not being constantly renewed by the Word of God will revert to the familiar; i.e., doing what we've always done, responding the way we've always responded, and getting what we've always gotten.

Those whose minds aren't renewed tend to be like chameleons. They can look the part and cater to prevailing modes, while on the inside they remain unchanged. Paul wrote to the Roman believers that God expects the believer's life to be directed and governed by the leading of His Spirit.

A comparison can be made between our spiritual and natural lives in that we're born, we're nurtured, we're taught, and we grow. Even if a child is raised by godly parents, the sinful nature within the child and the standards of this world will call to him or her to conform to a world system, a worldly mind-set, and a worldly mode of operation. Due to our inherent sinful nature, before we are born again of the Spirit of God, our inclinations are toward those things that oppose righteousness.

We are to guard against conformity to this world. To conform is to act in accordance with prevailing modes or customs. No matter how loudly the voices of this world cry out for us to embrace a system that calls wrong right and right wrong, we must always adhere to a higher standard. That standard must always be the Word of God, even when it's found to be unpopular. Most who conform find themselves doing so in order to be accepted and to avoid taking a position that conflicts with the majority. In some instances, this is referred to as being "politically correct."

The definition of transformation is to change the nature, function, or condition of something. When we are transformed, we are changed in our nature, function, and condition. Much like a steam engine transforming heat into energy, we are transformed from carnal to spiritual. This process happens by the renewing of our minds through the Word of God. The mind must be rewired. Our natural minds are wired to respond to the world and spirits that oppose the Kingdom of God. We can't receive the things of God, for they are foolishness to the natural man. "But the natural man does not receive the things of the Spirit of God, for they are foolishness to him; nor can he know them, because they are spiritually discerned" (1 Cor. 2:14).

Before we come to Christ, the only means of filtering incoming information is by processing it solely through our intellect based upon information given, perceived, and related to our past experiences and our knowledge base (what we've been taught). Given all of that, sometimes along with the input from others whom we might trust, we then proceed to act upon the information that has been presented to us. However, the Holy Ghost in the life of the believer adds a new dimension to each and every situation that we may face. We no longer have to rely solely upon what is presented to us in the natural, how our minds perceive it, what it looks like, sounds like, or what does or doesn't seem to make sense. The Holy Ghost will lead us around pitfalls in those situations where everything looks and sounds okay and others may be saying that all is well. We must learn to trust Him and to recognize His presence in our lives because there are times when everything looks good and all seems in order, but He gives us an unction within our spirit that says, "Something isn't right here. I know that it looks good and sounds good, but it's off." God's

Word has promised that the Spirit of God will lead the believer into all truth (John 16:13). He is a guide who has been called alongside to escort the believer through this life's journey. He shares with us the mind of Christ. The Spirit of God now serves as a filter, for He overrides the believer's intellect and frame of reference and is able to give vision and insight.

One can be blind physically and still have vision from God that allows him to have keen spiritual direction and awareness of the move of God. This is a vital part of the transformation process for the believer. We must walk by faith and not by sight. There is certainly a change in the nature of the child of God, which is an internal working of the Spirit of God. We don't just change our minds and decide to live for Christ, but what happens is supernatural. 1 Cor. 5:17 states, "If any man be in Christ Jesus he is a new creation, old things are passed away, behold all things have become new." Immediately upon our profession of faith, all things become new. We are new creatures. Our situations and circumstances may be the same, but a change occurs on the inside of each born-again believer. Although we may look the same, our inner man has been changed, and he's being renewed day by day as we're being transformed by the Spirit of God.

God begins to change our function, as our gifts, talents, and abilities are now to be used to advance the Kingdom of God. The condition of our heart changes as the oil of God's anointing begins to flow in our lives and to equip us for the work that He has assigned to our hands.

As you may recall, David didn't become king on the day that Samuel anointed him, yet we see that he was being transformed for the work that God had ordained for him to do long before Samuel showed up at his house. God was preparing his heart for His sheep and teaching him how to be a worshiper, as he would minister to the Lord while he was apart from the crowds. He learned the importance of intimacy with God and the responsibility of caring for the flocks before he was ushered into the place of overseeing God's people. It didn't matter what others thought; the oil of the anointing would not flow until David was in place. His heart had been prepared before the time of his transition, or coming forth, could occur.

Transition can only occur after we have been transformed by having our minds renewed through God's Word. This is the act, process, or instance of changing from one state, form, or place to another. The Lord is constantly repositioning us and transitioning us to a place where the oil of His anointing can flow freely in, through, and out of our lives. The oil flows in the place where we've been called. That is where our power and effectiveness lie! That is where our passion will meet its purpose!

The enemy wants us to see what we've always seen, but the Spirit of the Lord says, "Go back and look again. Keep looking until you see what I say is there." It doesn't matter what the natural eye and your senses tell you. What did God say? Turn away from every negative and destructive thought pattern, and choose to begin to see your circumstances in the light of God's Word. Any child of God who has a desire to please Him and who knows that God has made choice of them, must know that just because you're not the favorite one, it's no sign that you don't have the favor of God. There is so much talk about God's favor, and it truly exists, but to put it simply, it means that God is looking our way and that He is committed to our success. He has promised an expected end for us, and His thoughts toward us are always good (Jer. 29:11).

Transformation is a continual process that constantly turns the believer away from our old way of thinking and seeing things, while preparing us to transition to that place in God that our spirits long for. Our desire is to be cloaked with a greater anointing and transitioned into our next level of living for the King! This place in God is ours to have, but without transformation, there is no transition.

Moment of Reflection

So many of you have the heart and an anointing for the work of the Lord. Allow His Word to transform you, then watch His Spirit transition you to the place where His anointing will begin to flow in your life in ways that you never thought possible.

Grow in Grace

But grow in the grace and in the knowledge of our Lord and Savior Jesus Christ. To Him be the glory both now and forever. Amen.

2 Peter 3:18

We're to grow in grace and in the knowledge of Christ. Who is He? In Him dwells all of the fullness of the Godhead bodily (Col. 2:9). We're given of His Spirit in measure, but all that the Father is, all that the Son is, and all that's accessible through the Holy Ghost is in Jesus without measure. The three are one.

We're to know Him in the fellowship of His sufferings. During those times that we feel alone in trials and tests, He speaks to us. He gives strategies and solutions for working out our problems. By this, we come to know Him more intimately. Those who refuse or resist times of suffering are subject to becoming fickle and shallow because intimacy comes from times of testing and suffering with Him where only He can minister to us. We have fellowship with Him in sufferings.

We are to grow in knowledge as we grow in grace. We learn about Christian living and what grace entails, but we are to grow in our knowledge of Christ and His character. Knowledge is power. We cannot stop at learning about the Christian lifestyle. Christ has all wisdom, all power, and every devil in hell is subject to Him. The enemy knows that where there is no knowledge, there is no power. That's where the devil defeats us. We develop and nurture an intimate relationship with the Lord by reading His Word, praying, and fasting. In this way, we learn His character, His mind, and His heart.

In this day of great deception, where men seek their own wills rather than the will of God, we must have such an intimate knowledge of Him so that we are able to recognize His voice. We are warned in 2 Timothy 3:1 that in the last days, perilous times will come, and men will be lovers of themselves rather than lovers of God. That time is here. We must guard against being ensnared by such spirits that take captive those who rebel against the knowledge and will of God. The intimacy that accompanies the growth of a mature believer will cause him or her to recognize the move of God even in the midst of confusion.

We will experience more of God and His power as we lose more of ourselves. We must decrease, and He must increase. What is written on pages of the Bible must be taken into our spirits and applied to our lives through everyday experiences. We cannot access what we do not have knowledge of. As we grow in grace and in our knowledge of Him, we will be poised and ready for the next move of God. Remember that as believers, we have direct access to the throne room of God. Could it be that the Lord wants to reveal Himself to us more than we long to experience Him?

Moment of Reflection

Man seeks a full knowledge of God only to be frustrated in his search, for God is only revealed through His Son, Jesus.

Fortify!

And Jesus returned in the power of the Spirit into Galilee.

Luke 4:14

What do you find yourself doing when things seem to be going wrong and nothing appears to be working in your favor? If we're not careful, these are times that will cause us to become distracted. We may lose sight of the fact that all things work together for our good when we love God and are called according to His purpose. Therefore, we must stay focused in our deserts and valleys and use them as places of fortification just as Jesus did when He was driven into the wilderness. He resisted the attack of the devil by using the Word of God. The Bible says in Luke 4:14: "And Jesus returned in the power of the Spirit into Galilee; and there went out a fame of Him through all the region round about." The emphasis here is on the fact that after He endured much temptation in His wilderness experience, Jesus came out fortified in the power of the Spirit.

We are not warring against flesh and blood. Our battles are fought in the spirit realm, and we must build our spirit man up through God's Word in order to resist the devil in our "dry seasons," or "wilderness experiences." Jesus was driven into the wilderness by the Spirit of God, not by the devil (Matt. 4:1). This experience was not meant to destroy Him, but to strengthen and empower Him.

There will be seasons in our lives when the Lord will separate us from close friends and that which is familiar in order to bring focus and new direction to us. It is during these times that we come to grips with where we really are in our walk with the Lord. We must be determined to go to the next level and be willing to resist the devil's temptation for us to quit or to take the easy way out. In Luke 4:3-7, the devil offered Jesus several options, but none of them were in line with the will of the Father. This wilderness experience afforded Him the opportunity to make a decision to fulfill God's will, God's way. He didn't have to prove that He was the Son of God by turning stones to bread. He chose not to abort the plan of God by worshiping Satan in order to obtain the glory of the worldly kingdoms and the authority over them. He knew that all things exist in and through Him. He could not allow Satan to hand the victory to Him. All kingdoms and authority had to be conquered through His suffering and shed blood by way of the cross. Finally, He knew within Himself that all of heaven stood behind Him and that He didn't need to test or tempt God with trivial acts to invoke the intervention of the hosts of heaven. He knew who He was when He went into the wilderness, and that knowledge sustained Him. He is the living Word, and He was sustained and fortified by the spoken Word of God.

Wilderness experiences are used to fortify us. During these times, the enemy appears to be gaining on us and suppressing our ability to advance and to commune with God.

God will make provision for us, even in the dry places, if we will remember His Word and trust that He is able to perform His Word on our behalf. He will place a wall between us and the enemy, and although we may sense the presence of evil all around us, we will be shielded and hidden from the snare of the fowler. In spite of our circumstances, during these times, we are to fortify ourselves in the Spirit by feeding upon the Word of God and endeavoring to walk in its light.

The enemy's tactics never change. He comes only to steal, to kill, and to destroy. Although he may mask as an angel of light, there will never be another agenda when he presents himself. It is only through the power of God's Word that he is forced to flee from the presence and life of the believer. We can be certain that he will return after a season. Jesus said, "…for the prince of this world cometh, and hath nothing in me" John 14:30. When he comes, he looks for growth on the deposit that he has placed in our lives. Refuse to yield to him. Give no place to his seed of deception. Resist him steadfast in the faith. Our enemy, Satan, doesn't want us to use the weaponry that the Lord has given to us because he knows that when we use it, strongholds are going to come down, the captive are going to be set free, and Christ will be exalted!

We must use what we have at our disposal. God has placed a sword in the hand of the believer, which is His Word and a testimony upon our lips, which no man can refute. Every believer has a testimony of God's grace, mercy, and forgiveness in his or her life. In times of testing, we must reflect on the great things that God has already done. These times of reflection give us the strength and desire to go forward and to trust our Lord in a much greater way.

We must use our "desert seasons" to fortify ourselves. We must get on our faces before God and cry out for a closer walk with Him. Although the enemy pursues and seeks to destroy us, he is overcome. 1 John 5:4 states: "For whatsoever is born of God overcometh the world; and this is the victory that overcometh the world, even our faith." Our spirit man is strengthened, or fortified, along the journey to enable us to go another round with the enemy and to build the faith of others. Realize that the Word of God is the primary part of our spiritual weaponry when we're under the enemy's attack. Study it, learn it, and use it!

Moment of Reflection

The dry place has not been allowed in your life to kill you, but to cause you to thirst after God and to hunger after the "living bread."

Choose Abundant Life Now

The thief cometh not, but for to steal, and to kill, and to destroy; I am come that they might have life, and that they might have it more abundantly.

John 10:10

To choose is a must. God has given all of us the autonomy to choose between blessing and cursing, as well as life and death. Choose life! What are we choosing as we choose life? We're choosing to forgive, to loose those who don't mean us well or who bring frustration to our lives. We are choosing to do God's will, His way.

Choosing abundant life means we must choose to devote quality time with the Lord and to share with confidence those things that He gives us to share. We must choose to boldly do the things that He leads us to do. Many times others may not agree with God's plan for us, and we may not always understand the path that He would have us to take. Our choice must always be to obey and to trust that all things will work together for our good. Things may not look good when we start, and different elements of our lives may seem to be totally disconnected from one another, but they will "work together" and "for our good" when we love the Lord and are called according to His purpose (Rom. 8:28).

Isn't that what it's all about? His purpose. No longer our wills, but His will must be done in and through our lives. We make the choice to lay aside our plans and say yes to God's will, knowing that He has a plan for our lives that will bring glory to Himself. The working of His will in our lives brings edification to the body of Christ and satisfaction and joy to our lives like nothing that we could have ever planned for ourselves. We may not ever be rich by the world's standard, and many may never know our names. However, we can have the assurance that the Lord knows who we are, where we are, and He will prosper our way. Prosperity doesn't always carry dollar signs with it, although it can. The question is, Can we have abundant life without an abundance of financial wealth?

One of the greatest detriments to the body of believers who seek to live abundant and prosperous lives is the pervasive mind-set within Christian circles that God intends for all of His people to be rich. We're to be rich in grace, in His mercy, and in His anointing. We should seek to have these things abounding in our lives. Money may come, but if it doesn't, that is no indication that we're not favored of God or that we're of no use to His Kingdom. If the abundant life were all about money, we would have nothing to share with others about the abundant life in Christ unless our bank accounts were overflowing. The Lord is faithful to perform His Word, and He will supply all of our needs according to His riches in glory by Christ Jesus (Phil. 4:19). We will lack no good thing because He will withhold no good thing from them who walk upright before Him. Contrary to what some may choose to believe, everyone will not experience financial wealth. There are numerous and varied reasons for this but one thing is certain, Jesus said, "the poor you have with you always" (Matt. 26:11; John 12:8). In context of the Scripture, Jesus spoke these words after His disciples became indignant at the woman who came and poured precious and costly ointment on Jesus' head while He sat at meat in the house of Simon the leper. Their expressed concern was that the ointment could have been put to better use by being sold and giving the money to the poor. What Jesus was stressing in that instance was relationship and the fact that the woman had perceived the importance of ministering to Jesus as opposed to holding onto her ointment, which had only temporal value.

I am certainly not advocating that Christians should be poor. Everything belongs to our God. Many in the world tend to think that the Christian life should reflect lack and struggle, but the Lord has come to give us life and that more abundantly. Those who are called by the name of Christ should never contend for riches, but earnestly contend for the faith, contend for the Kingdom of God and His righteousness. We must get back to proclaiming what Paul advocated in Philippians 4:11: "I have learned, in whatsoever state I am, therewith to be content." When this becomes our priority, all that we need and the majority of all that we could ever want will be added unto us.

Abundant life is about seeking Christ and not possessions. When we allow ourselves to equate the riches of this world with the blessings of God, we run the risk of looking upon those with less as though they've "missed the mark" or "lack the fullness of Christ." While this may be the attitude in many Christian circles, it is a spirit of error that is contrary to the teachings of Christ. We must resist this type of spirit within the body of Christ, for the Lord has a way of taking one down to put up another. He has a way of pulling His people from the background to the forefront without the approval of men.

These are the true riches of God: to be able to walk in His anointing, to be sensitive to His Spirit, and to be able to find our place within the body of Christ and to be effective there. As we walk in the way and will of God, we can't help but to prosper because God has ordained it so. He has decreed that blessings will overtake us, but I maintain that one of the greatest gifts that we can possess is to experience the true gratification that comes from being in His will and walking in His Spirit.

The life of abundance that has been promised to the believer is never to be measured by the things that one may or may not possess. Things will come as we pursue our God! Things apart from a true relationship with Christ have little meaning. Within our society, there are so many people who have more money than they could ever spend, and yet they are not satisfied, nor do they enjoy fulfilled lives.

Our news media are replete with those of prominence and affluence who have taken their lives and the lives of their loved ones while seemingly being at the pinnacle of life. With all of the substance that they possessed, why were they not satisfied? We were created for fellowship with our Lord, and only within the context of our lives being in harmony with His will do we find true peace and contentment. The peace and contentment of the believer stems from the knowledge that our lives are hidden in Christ. We have the assurance that the Lord is in control and will go before us in every situation. He has your back!

Many have faced much difficulty and hurt in this life, and they just can't seem to grasp that there is a loving, caring God, who is interested in them. They certainly don't feel a part of anything connected minutely with abundance, except, of course, abundance of pain, rejection, humiliation, etc. Out of much pain great good can be realized. We can choose to ask the Lord to change our hearts, to heal our hurts, and to use our negative experiences for the good of others and the upbuilding of the Kingdom of God. Many have suffered what we've suffered, but somehow when we go through our pain, we're convinced that we're the only ones who have ever experienced such. Not true! God's Word states in 1 Corinthians 10:13, "There hath no temptation taken you but such as is common to man." It's common! Others have encountered what you are now dealing with. That same Scripture in the New Living Translation reads, "The temptations in your life are no different from what others experience. And God is faithful. He will not allow the temptation to be more than you can stand. When you are tempted, He will show you a way out so that you can endure." Refuse to exist in a vacuum. Make the choice to live!

Break forth and begin to declare the Lord's greatness. Refuse to be bound! There is no one else like Him. He heals all of our diseases and makes the crooked paths straight. The Lord doesn't only do miracles, but He is the very essence of the miraculous! By His Word the worlds were framed. He caused something from nothing. He is eternal, has no beginning and no end. Our human minds can't comprehend this, so we must grasp it by faith, knowing that which He has prepared and ordained for our lives will be brought to pass in spite of what we do or do not have/what we can or cannot see.

As odd as it may seem, God tends to turn our situations around as we turn our attention away from ourselves and begin to focus our attention on helping others to live, to be delivered, and to be set free.

While freeing others, we somehow find ourselves radically freed as well. Others are hurting and need to hear what you have to say. God wants to heal us and bring abundance not only to us individually, but to those around us who are masked and are just waiting for someone to speak up and say, "Hey, I'm hurting, too!"

The truly abundant life never has been and never will be measured by the things that a man or woman possesses, but by who possesses that man or that woman. To live in Christ is to have access to a wealth of joy, peace, understanding, and pleasure that's not dictated by our station in life (see Rom. 14:17).

We can enjoy an abundant life now! Choose not to complain, but to see yourself as Christ sees you: delivered, healed, useful, special, unique, ever becoming what He has ordained you to be. Choose never to sum your life up based upon the sum of things that you possess because life's circumstances can change in an instant. Our God is in control, and He has great plans that He intends to fulfill in your life—your abundant life!

Moment of Reflection

The choice is yours to be all that God has purposed for you to be, and once you do that, no one has the power to stop the will of God that is at work in your life!

Maximizing Your Potential

My substance was not hid from thee, when I was made in secret, and curiously wrought in the lowest parts of the earth.

Psalm 139:15

From childhood, we all have inclinations, desires, and dreams. Some dreams stem from the expressed desires that others have for us because of something that they may have seen in us. That something is called potential, which, by definition, means "possible but not yet realized; capable of being but not yet in existence; latent." Potential is not tangible. It may exist, but can't be handled or experienced in any way. There is so much in us that is capable of being, yet for many reasons may lie dormant.

After our spirits have been made alive in Christ, we begin to experience a pull toward our godly potential. God is concerned about every facet of our lives. He will help us to bring to reality that within us which is capable of being but is not yet existent. If we refuse to act on what is not yet evident, we will not experience change, although everything that we need is available to us in its potential state. God wants our potential not only to be realized, or brought to fruition, but to be maximized. To maximize something means to make it as great as possible.

Hebrews 4:2 lets us know that the Word of God is of no profit, if not mixed with faith. "For unto us was the gospel preached, as well as unto them: but the word preached did not profit them, not being mixed with faith in them that heard it." Do you believe that God has a place for you, can reveal it to you, and then bring it to pass? He is more than able to do it as He now pulls you toward your godly potential. The root word in potential is "potent," which is defined as possessing inner or physical strength; powerful.

There's something in each of us that God wants to bring out. Only He can do it! Only He knows the fullness of our potential. There is a process that we must go through in order to become who God wants us to be. It won't always be easy, and we won't always understand what He is doing. This process constantly pushes us to that place in our spiritual walk where we become so pregnant with potential that we realize that we must deliver or die. In order for God to get the glory in our lives, what is in us must come out. It must be birthed!

For those of us who have had a child or who look forward to doing so, we realize that there is a process that we must go through in order for our potential to be mothers to become a reality. We must go through something if we choose to bring a child into this world.

Labor is no fun, but women keep going through it for the joy that comes after. All sorts of experiences are available for those going through the birthing process. We can use a birthing room, where the entire family is welcome to participate in the experience, we can choose to sit in a pool of water that is designed to make the process more expedient and natural, or we may choose to stay at home and have a midwife to assist us. No matter what means is chosen, the reality is that there will be labor before a delivery, or birth, takes place. There is a point in labor where a woman loses herself. She is no longer counting, no longer paying attention to how many breaths she needs to take, etc. All that she knows is that it's time for what has been growing inside of her to come out, and even in her tired state, she uses all of her remaining energy to push in order to expel the reality of that which for so long was only potential.

Just as it is in the natural, so it is in the spirit. If we want that thing of power, that potent thing in us, to be birthed, we must become tenacious. We must allow the Spirit of God to take us to the point in this birthing process where we lose ourselves. We must get to the point where we are willing to bring forth by any means necessary. Our attitude must be, deliver or die. That thing of potential in us must come forth and begin to live.

Even knowing the pain and the long hours of labor, women continue to have children. Many will go through the process several times, and when their youngest gets to a certain age, they begin to desire more children. In John 16:21, we read, "A woman when she is in travail hath sorrow, because her hour is come: but as soon as she is delivered of the child, she remembereth no more the anguish, for joy that a man is born into the world." When we get to where God is taking us, the pain of the process won't seem so bad. We will know beyond all doubt that it was well worth it, and we will thank God for it.

The Spirit of the Lord says to us today, "When you start believing what you say about Me, then I'll start doing what you boast that I can do, and I will be to you who you say that I am."

Moment of Reflection

Recognize that potential lies within each of us. Acknowledge the Lord in all of your ways, and close the door on doubt, fear, unbelief, and every work of the flesh. Take hold of God with tenacity and choose to believe Him regardless of what it looks like. Refuse to panic, for this is not of the Spirit. Remember that birthing is a process.

Frontline Living

For we wrestle not against flesh and blood, but against principalities, against powers, against the rulers of the darkness
of this world, against spiritual wickedness in high places.

Ephesians 6:12

We must make a conscious decision to walk in the ways of
God, to be a part of His army, and to allow Him to have
control, or lordship, of our lives. There was a period in my life when
I served in the armed forces. This entitled me to wear a uniform that
identified me as a member of the Air Force. When I received orders
to change assignments, whether in the United States or abroad, all of
my travel expenses were covered by the United States government.
Part of my benefits included being able to live on military installa-
tions, where costs related to housing were also covered. Wherever
my family lived, there were always people who hung around the
military but who weren't connected in any way. Some lived in the
city where the military installation was located, and others came
into contact with us while they were vacationing in the immediate

area. Since they weren't a part of the military, they weren't able to partake in the privileges afforded to military families.

We can use this same type of analogy when speaking of our commitment to Christ. Unlike with the military, we don't commit to serve the Lord for short periods of time (although this is the reality of what happens in some cases). Our commitment to the Lord is meant to be for our lifetime here and hereafter. We're to serve the Lord for the entirety of our lives. After we commit to the Lord, we realize through His Word that He has a plan and a purpose for our lives. We must be about His business, and there is no time to waste. The steps of a righteous man or woman are ordered by the Lord, and He chooses to lead us throughout the course of our lives according to the plan that He prepared for us before our lives on earth began.

There is a vast difference between being sent on assignment and being on vacation. When we are on assignment, our mind-set is different. We realize that we're not on location to carry out our own agendas; rather, we have an assignment and mission from the Lord to fulfill. There are individual assignments, and there are those that are tied to and affect the entire group to which we are connected.

After we say yes to the will of the Lord, by accepting Him as our Savior and Lord, we are changed and are enlisted in His service for the advancement of the Kingdom of God. We soon learn that we are engaged in spiritual warfare and that we now oppose that which we once lived and fought for during much of our lives.

Spiritual weaponry is issued to us, and we are covered and protected in all that we are assigned to do for the Kingdom. The sad reality is that many are just hanging around the church and handling the things of God as though they're on vacation. Since they are oblivious to the warfare that is being waged all around them in the spirit, the enemy uses them for target practice. He knows that they have a form of godliness but no power. When spiritual battles arise, they respond with carnal or fleshly weapons. A "vacation" mentality on the frontline is detrimental for the entire unit. We have to stay alert and be aware of the enemy's tactics at all times.

Being on the frontline means understanding that our very lives are an assignment with missions attached. The Bible lets us know that everyone serves a master. We carry out the assignments and desires of whoever we choose to yield ourselves to, but we will serve somebody. Jesus spoke to the Jews in John 8:34 and told them that "Whosoever committeth sin is the servant of sin," and He further stated in verse 44, "You are of your father, the devil and the lusts of your father ye will do." This wasn't due to the fact that they were Jews, but due to whose purpose and plan they had chosen to carry out and to be subject to. This applies to any of us who choose to reject the testimony of Jesus and choose rather to walk in unbelief.

Saul was on assignment from the devil until he was knocked off of his beast on the Damascus road. The disciples had sense enough to know that he was a threat to them and the cause of Christ if God had not truly delivered him as they had heard. Therefore, they were somewhat justified in being leery of him immediately following the news of his conversion.

Some of us have chosen to abort certain missions because of what it looks like or because it seems that no one is supporting us. Others have said that what God has given us to do can't be done, so we've walked away from the task.

Frontline living requires that we be willing to follow orders regardless of what the situation looks like. We must be born of the Spirit of God in order to receive the things of God. The things of God are foolishness to them that are lost, to them that are perishing. Jesus chose the twelve disciples, and one of them was a devil. He knew it from the start, so why did He do it? It may seem foolish to some because He knew what He was getting into, but He did it because it was in God's plan. He had come to do the will of the Father.

The natural man cannot receive the things of God. God doesn't relate to our flesh, nor does He seek to appeal to our flesh. Much of what He instructs you and me to do won't make sense to our natural minds, but we must remember that He is all-knowing. Because He is eternal, He knows the end of all things from the beginning. What He is doing in our lives at any given time may have nothing to do with the present, but perhaps it has more to do with where we will be in two, five, or even ten years from now. Our God moves and speaks from eternity, affecting change in time.

Frontline living will require that spiritual weaponry be issued to us and that we be trained to use it. The weapons of our warfare are not carnal, but are mighty through God to the pulling down of strongholds. Many boast of being "bad" in the world, but the physical weapons of the world are ineffective in the Kingdom of God. Spirits are not affected or subdued by bullets, knives, or grenades. You can kill a murdering terrorist, but after he or she is dead, the spirit of murder still exists and has an effect on the minds and faculties of those who will yield to it. Ephesians 6:12 states, "We wrestle not against flesh and blood, but against principalities, against powers, against the rulers of the darkness of this world, against spiritual wickedness in high places." Placing weapons in the hands of children or those who have not been trained in their proper use spells certain disaster. Likewise, those who are on the frontline as it relates to the things of God must be mature and must have an understanding of the power and proper use of the weapons that are a part of the arsenal of the believer. This comes by immersing ourselves in God's Word and trusting Him when He allows us to go through various tests that require the use of faith, prayer, fasting, and walking in truth and righteousness while remaining secure under the helmet of salvation.

Believers are citizens of the Kingdom of God who are sent by God to this world as ambassadors. Wherever He has sent us and whatever mission He has assigned to us, the Kingdom takes responsibility to cover all related expenses. We are covered by the blood of Christ, and that is better than any life insurance policy that this world could provide.

When we're living on the frontline, we are totally exposed. We can't be afraid to die. This doesn't only relate to physical death, but spiritual as well. We must be willing to die daily. Romans 8:12 states, "Therefore, brethren, we are debtors, not to the flesh, to live after the flesh." We owe nothing to our past, which was wrought by the works of the flesh, and we must stop protecting it. We can now mortify, or kill, the deeds of the body through the Spirit of God and live. Those on the frontline must be willing to expose the devil and the work that he wrought in our lives in the past, for we have been set free. When we hide, cover up, and protect our flesh, we are bound, gagged, and restricted in our ability to make war on the enemy. Christ has come to set us free. The weaponry that has been issued for those who live on the frontline provides no protection for those who retreat. We must be on the offensive. We must penetrate the enemy's camp.

Moment of Reflection

Child of God, we are not here on vacation! Take up your weapons and boldly carry out each assignment that the King has given to you. Remember that all of heaven is backing you!

God Is Looking for You

(This writing was inspired by Everett Silver, Jr.)

But the hour cometh, and now is, when the true worshippers shall worship the Father in spirit and in truth: for the Father seeketh such to worship Him.

John 4:23

The prerequisite for handling or ministering to God's people is that we first love Him. He came to Peter with a question that had to do with ministry but was all about relationship. The question was, "Peter, do you love Me?" or, "Lovest thou Me?" Three times Peter was asked this question. The Lord didn't ask: "Do you love my people? Will you commit to praying for them, fasting for them? Will you be patient with them and forgiving toward them?" No, the question was, "Lovest thou Me?" because the true test that must be passed before one is commissioned for work in God's Kingdom is that we love the King. Then and only then are we qualified to feed or otherwise tend His sheep. It is because we love the King that we can be entrusted to endure, to intercede, to build up, and to love God's sheep, His people, through hard times.

None of us should have to prove that we have a place in ministry when we know that God has called us. He will open doors for us that no man can shut. He will send for us at the appointed time, and He will place us in that spot that has been carved out just for us to fill.

He seeks those who are often rejects in the eyes of men but who are willing to come to Him without pretense and to lay all of their shortcomings at His feet. It's from this state of transparency and nakedness that He begins to clothe us with His Spirit. The more that we're willing to take off in terms of that which tends to exalt us in the flesh—our reliance on our looks, our dress, how well we may preach, teach or sing—the more He has an opportunity to be exalted in our lives. The Lord needs vessels who aren't afraid to be poured out and broken so that others may be restored and revived. The oil of the Spirit that has been poured into these earthen vessels was never meant to be stored up and used solely among other believers.

Our ministry to each other within the body of Christ is always that of edifying and equipping so that we may be useful in our mission to go out to the masses. We're called to those who are lost so that they may be won to Christ. It's a tragedy when so many are poised to be "sent," but few want to be prepared to go. We should earnestly desire all that God has promised us. We must be steadfast and willing to wait for that which He has allowed us to glimpse in the Spirit, rather than insisting that it manifest without delay. In other words, this is a race that must be run with patience; it is not a race of speed.

Wait upon the Lord and be of good courage, for He has need of you. If you have a heart toward God, He's looking for you. If you seek to worship Him in spirit and in truth, He seeks such to worship Him. You may not have wealth to reach the masses, but you can touch countless lives with your heart because a heart that is inclined toward God will lift others on the wings of prayer and catapult them into a dimension in God that surpasses all expectations. The heart of love and fervency will cause you to loose the bands of wickedness in the lives of many and to bring freedom and a song to souls that are oppressed. This can only be accomplished through those whose hearts and lives are linked and intertwined with the heart of the King. His heartbeat must become our heartbeat. This means that we have the compassion and caring that He has for all souls. His passion will become our passion, and His mind, our mind. We will desire to see souls saved, delivered, and set free by the power of God. Then, His mission will be our mission. The ultimate mission of God is that His Kingdom would be established in the earth and that His will would be done in earth as it is in heaven.

Moment of Reflection

"Also I heard the voice of the Lord, saying, Whom shall I send, and who will go for Us?" (Isa. 6:8a). Jesus willingly came forth from the Father. Jesus has asked us to go into all of the world for Him. What will your answer be?

No Longer Under the Circumstances

And hath raised us up together, and made us sit together in heavenly places in Christ Jesus . . .

Ephesians 2:6

We've all heard the saying "I'm doing all right under the circumstances." I submit to you today that the Lord has called His saints to live above and in spite of the circumstances that life may present to us. We are more than conquerors regardless of what is happening in our lives, for this is our place in God spiritually. Our position in Christ is not negatively affected by what we may be going through. Even when it appears that we're under, we're prevailing by the power and authority of the Spirit of the living God. There is no failure or lack in Him.

God is at work in our lives, even when it appears that there's no movement in our camp and it seems that God has looked away from our direction. We must begin to speak life over ourselves when no prophetic voices are speaking about the great move of God in our lives. We must stop waiting for others to validate the God in us. The true prophetic voice (the voice of the Spirit within us) can speak out of nothingness, emptiness, and desolation, for He sees where the natural eye can't see. Where others see abandon and lack, the Spirit of God helps us to see His choicest blessings in abundance while we're in the dry place. We're sustained by our fellowship with the most high God.

Although circumstances in our lives may seem contrary, our spiritual position is above and not beneath. We're the head and not the tail. We're seated in heavenly places in Christ Jesus (see Eph. 2:6). Some have said that we should "go where we're celebrated and not just tolerated." That sounds wonderful and gets a lot of "amens" when it's quoted, but someone has to be willing to stay the course and raise the tolerance level during those times when it is apparent that we're not the favorite one. Don't be thrown by fits of celebration because one day the crowds cried "Hosanna" to Jesus, and shortly thereafter, they were shouting, "Crucify Him!" The ways of men are sometimes quite fickle!

When we are called, we can no longer waste time looking for a platform from which to "do" ministry. We must understand that our lives are ministry. Whether or not people celebrate us, our task as saints is to effect change in the earth. We must remember that our steps are ordered by the Lord and what we sometimes encounter as negative situations or circumstances are really no more than tests that have been allowed by God to come our way. These tests help to sharpen and strengthen us.

At times it may seem as though people are holding you back, pushing you aside, and locking you away in a place of isolation. However, we can determine to view our circumstance from the vantage point of being seated with Christ in heavenly places. Things then will appear much differently. We will not find ourselves operating from the mind-set of being under our circumstances. They will not appear so great and overbearing. We will be able to ask the Lord to share with us His perspective on the situation so that we may respond appropriately.

No one has the power to prevent or stop that which God has ordained for your life. Don't be so concerned about finding a venue where you can stand and deliver the Word or bring a message. When we begin to think of our lives as ministry, we will realize that our words carry the power of life or death, blessing or cursing, whether we speak them from a pulpit in an auditorium filled with believers or in the marketplace.

We're taught at a young age to look to others for approval. It gives us a sense that we're doing the right thing, moving in the right direction when others approve of our decisions and choices. I ask, "whose approval do you need now? Who do you need to have cheering for you this time?" These are important questions because if those people can't see what God has shown to you or don't agree with the moves that you feel led to make, they could be keeping you from some very important areas of ministry if you're catering to their applause and approval.

What do you do when your enemy is relentless and faces you at every turn? What do you do when you feel their fiery darts whenever you're in their presence? Just as David did, we must resolve to walk in integrity. He was certainly chosen by God and he was anointed to rule over God's people, yet his circumstances in and outside of the home were bleak. Family had overlooked him, and now Saul sought to kill him on several occasions. Oftentimes people will hate us without a cause or because of the threat that they may perceive that we pose to them, their position, or their status. It's usually about status, influence and perceived encroachment upon territories that will cause people to lash out at us. Saul's perception was that because the people cheered and celebrated David, there was nothing left but for David to overtake the kingdom. In other words, Saul thought "he has stolen the hearts of the people, what's left but for him to overtake the throne also." This was not in David's heart but it was Saul's perception which ultimately caused him to respond from a position of being under the circumstance as he saw it.

David's response was to walk in integrity (above the circumstances) and to place the circumstances under the authority of God by refusing to touch God's anointed one. This allowed the Lord to bring resolve to the matter.

We all want to be celebrated at some level. However, God is calling for someone to be steadfast and to raise the tolerance level. Although we're not celebrated, we must choose to say what the Bible says even when we're not celebrated where we've been placed to serve. The bible says that in the last days many will not endure sound doctrine but will turn away to those who will tell them what they want to hear.

God can and will plant our feet as hinds feet so that we may be able to dwell in the high and sometimes challenging places without fear of harm. We desire to respond to life's challenges from a higher place, no longer living by the dictates of or under our circumstances.

Moment of Reflection

Perhaps you don't really need the Lord to change or to remove those difficult circumstances in your life today, but to share His perspective or vantage point with you. Remember you are seated with Him in heavenly places NOW. Ask Him to help you to see your circumstances from that vantage point.

Higher Heights in God

I press toward the mark for the prize of the high calling of
God in Christ Jesus.

Philippians 3:14

We each must choose between higher heights in God or
high esteem in the eyes of men, deeper depths in God or
an appearance and reputation for being "deep" in the eyes of the
people. Men can help to develop our talents, but unless God infuses,
endows, and breathes His anointing on them, they will be no more
than just good talents. Granted, talent can take us a long way, but
talent can never deliver, set free, or destroy the yokes of the devil.
For this, we need the anointing of God. Our gifts will make room
for us and take us before great men, but the anointing of God will
determine what we do once we're established in the "large" place.
The cry of many has been, "Lord, enlarge my territory," but we must
understand that our territories are enlarged so that the Kingdom of
God may be advanced.

Before our territories are enlarged, we must come into agreement with the will of God as it pertains to what we're called to do in

the earth. We must pray for the heart of God and the mind of Christ (Rom. 8:7; 1 Cor. 2:16; John 15:15). The New Testament shares a lot with us about the relationship that the disciples had with Jesus, but the only thing that it records them having asked Him to teach them was how to pray (Luke 11:1). They saw Him pray often, and they knew that John the Baptist had taught his disciples to pray. They must have realized that there is much power to be obtained through the art and privilege of prayer.

When we pray, we must always expect that our prayers will be answered, and we must know beyond a shadow of a doubt that God hears us. Jesus said in John 11:41, "Father, I thank thee that thou hast heard me. And I know that thou hearest me always." So it is with the believer. God desires to take us higher, but we must always approach Him with confidence and the knowledge that He hears us. His desire is to see His greatest good perfected in us.

The believer must always seek a more intimate and higher place of fellowship with our Lord. It's ours to attain, for the Word of God declares, "Draw nigh to God, and He will draw nigh to you" (James 4:8). Intimacy with the Lord is not a by-product of salvation. Intimacy must be cultivated through times of prayer, fasting, and meditation upon His Word.

In order to obtain a closer walk with the Lord and attain our next level in our relationship with Him, we must be willing to be flexible, or pliable. If we say that God can use us in any way that He chooses, then we must mean it! Hold to the assurance that God is in control. He's in our tomorrows, and He has a divine plan for each of our lives.

There is constant change around us, and at times, this causes anxiety. We see others progressing, while we're aging and doors in our lives may not seem to be opening. No matter what stage of life we may find ourselves in, God still wants to use us and can use us. History shows that He has never called out and used the most qualified, but those who are simply available. The lives of the victorious saints have always been about attaining higher heights in God as opposed to obtaining high esteem in the eyes of men.

There are always higher heights to attain in the things of God and in our relationship with Him. Endeavor to draw nigh unto Him, and He has promised that as you do this, He will draw nigh unto you.

Moment of Reflection

Have you become discouraged as it appears that others around you are making progress, while your life, your ministry, and your walk with the Lord have become somewhat stagnant? You can walk as close to the Lord as you choose.

Author and Finisher of Our Faith

(Faith Walkers)

Looking unto Jesus the author and finisher of our faith; who for the joy that was set before Him endured the cross despising the shame, and is set down at the right hand of the throne of God.

Hebrews 12:2

God has called us to be "faith walkers." How often do you think about that? All that we do must be done through, because of, and with faith. "For we walk by faith and not by sight" (2 Cor. 5:7); "the just shall live by faith" (Hab. 2:4; Rom. 1:17); "for without faith it is impossible to please Him for he who comes to God must believe that He is, and that He is a rewarder of those who diligently seek Him" (Heb.11:6); "for by grace are ye saved through faith" (Eph. 2:8); "for whatsoever is not of faith is sin" (Rom. 14:23b). These are just a few of many Scriptures that give a road map for the life of the believer and how we are to live. There's no other way to walk the Christian walk except by faith.

Just because we feel that we're lacking in faith doesn't mean that we are. Faith goes beyond feeling and isn't dictated by or gauged by feelings. As a matter of fact, God's Word lets us know that when we're weak (in our own resources), then are we strong. God's strength is made perfect in weakness (2 Cor. 12:9). We must look to Him, for He is the Author and Finisher of our faith (Hebrews 12:2a). Well, what does this mean, exactly? In its simplest form, the faith that we possess came from Him, and all of the faith that we will ever need in order to accomplish that which has been assigned to our hand will be given by God without lack. He will finish whatever He has begun in us!

We must not shrink back because of doubt, fear, or unbelief. These three are generally found operating together, and they have a way of slipping into our lives whenever we begin to look at ourselves and our limited capabilities, resources, talents, connections, etc. We must continue to look to Jesus and not to ourselves, our friends, our bank accounts, or our jobs. He has promised to supply all of our needs, not according to any of these things, but by His riches in glory. Therefore, the supply will be more than enough.

Be convinced that Jesus will do all that He has promised, and be confident in your expectation of Him to do it. All of our needs shall be met! Therefore, it doesn't matter what the bank statement says or what the checkbook looks like; we can expect that our needs will be met.

Continue to hope in God. We must oftentimes encourage ourselves in the Lord because circumstances will turn bleak and acquaintances will run out of answers for our situations. But if we can continue to have hope, then the Lord has a means to operate on our behalf. He will stir our faith toward those things that He has purposed for our lives. Hope in God maketh not ashamed (Ps. 25:3). Faith will give substance to our hope; otherwise, we're operating in nothing more than "wishful thinking." Faith is the substance of things hoped for; therefore, our hope in God goes far beyond just a wish. "I wish that God would come through for me," or, "I wish that God would do this or that." By faith we're able to stand in agreement with God's Word and believe Him to show Himself strong in our situations. He is concerned about what concerns us (1 Pet. 5:6-7).

Even "faith walkers" can become confused or even beset (which is to be derailed in a sense, or thrown off track) in our faith because we've been taught that we can pray our desires to the Lord and He has to answer according to our desires. When the outcome isn't what we've sought the Lord for or have waited for, we're suddenly disheartened because it seems that the Word of God hasn't "worked" for us. It may seem that God hasn't come through on His Word. We begin to question, sometimes openly, but oftentimes within ourselves, where no one knows the torment and doubt with which we contend. There are saints who are powerful in ministry, anointed, and gifted who inwardly struggle with the "whys" of seemingly unanswered prayers. There are many saved individuals who truly love the Lord who have had to battle with disappointment after praying for loved ones or members of their congregations for healings, only to see them die. Many times others within the body have been too quick to say, "Well, they just didn't have the faith to believe as they should have." No, I'm convinced that just as the case was with Paul, who sought the Lord three times to have the thorn removed from his flesh, there will be times in our lives when the Lord's response to us will be that His grace alone must be sufficient for us. The sovereign will of God must always supersede the desires of man. Each of us will face hard and difficult times in our lives, but our total surrender to the sovereignty of God will allow us to say yes to His will, even when we don't understand it. This is the true test of the believer!

It isn't about how many are healed when you pray, but where do you stand when the answer doesn't come the way that you thought it would? Can you still believe God? Can you still profess His Word with confidence?

I certainly struggled with this when my mother was diagnosed with cancer shortly after my father's sudden death from a heart attack in October 1995. The Lord had allowed me to lead both of my parents and my two older sisters to the Lord prior to my father's death. Needless to say, when my mother received the diagnosis, we were all initially devastated, but soon rebounded and made it our mission to only speak faith, to share faith-building materials with our mother, and to have her receive prayer from those who believed in the power of God to heal. We were convinced that cancer didn't have to be a death sentence; rather, we were determined to see God move on her behalf. We all read Scriptures that pertained to faith and God's will to heal us. My oldest sister shared a book with my mother that was written by Mrs. Betty Price, the wife of Dr. Frederick K.C. Price, a prominent faith teacher, who had been healed from cancer, and we sought out other faith-building resources as well. We had various ones praying for her via prayer requests, and we were trusting that God would raise her up. On November 16, 1998, she went home to be with the Lord, and needless to say, this was one of the most trying times during my walk with the Lord. This was a most difficult faith walk. What had gone wrong? My faith was severely challenged, and the enemy tried to take my mind. It's hard to talk with anyone who hasn't experienced the pain and loss of a parent, particularly a mother who had been so very close, a friend, a confidant, and finally, a dear sister in Christ. I purposefully stayed away from those who were of the persuasion that when prayers aren't answered our way, it's our fault. I was mature enough in the Word of God to know that God has the last say and that His ways are not our ways. I wasn't about to allow others to put a guilt trip on me about my mother's death. I had seen that played out too many times before in the lives of others. The words of consolation that many tried to use that indicated that God had given the "ultimate healing" didn't sit well with me, either. God's Word is very clear regarding death. It is an enemy, and, in fact, 1 Cor. 15:26 states that "the last enemy that shall be destroyed is death." I really began to seek God in earnest and to pour my heart out to Him. After all, I'm called to minister to others, and if I can't say with confidence that my God heals, then there's lack in my ministry. After months of grief and many nights crying bitter tears, I was led to the portion of Scripture wherein Shadrach, Meshach, and Abednego were thrown into a fiery furnace after choosing to serve the true and living God and refusing to bow to the image of an idol (Dan. 3:17-18). Their answer to the king was, "If it be so, our God whom we serve is able to deliver us from the burning fiery furnace, and He will deliver us out of thine hand, O King" (v. 17). "But if not, be it known unto thee, O King, that we will not serve thy gods, nor worship the golden image which thou hast set up" (v. 18). They had confidence in the all-powerful God as the "finisher of their faith." He had begun their walk of faith, and now it was up to Him to carry it out to completion—whatever His will was for the ending. In the midst of their time of great testing, they were able to declare that no matter what their God decided to do, they knew that He was able to deliver them. During my trial, this passage spoke volumes to me, although I had read it many times before. God chooses what He'll do and when, but our faith must always stand fast in the knowing that He's able to do all things, whether He chooses to or not. It's His prerogative to heal or not. All souls are His, and each of us has an appointment with death that we must keep; we cannot break it. For "it is appointed unto men once to die, but after this the judgment" (Heb. 9:27).

As you make this journey of faith, just know that whatever you're faced with, God has allowed it to be so, and He will bring you out victoriously. Stay away from those who present themselves as allies but who oppose your faith and who speak contrary to the Word of God. Remember that He is the Author and Finisher of our faith. He has called you, and only He knows what it's going to take to get you to where He's taking you.

Are you wrestling with anything in your life now where it appears God has let you down or didn't come through for you? Believe me, you're not alone. But remember, you're called to be a "faith walker." Take the time to talk with God about your thoughts, feelings, hurts, anger, and the bitterness that you may be experiencing. Allow His cleansing power to work in and through your life as He releases to you a new wave of power and anointing. We must be free in our spirits in order to be effective witnesses and ministers to others. God loves you, and whatever has come your way, even if the enemy brought it and meant it for evil, God has promised to use it to accomplish good as the end result.

It's easy for others to misread signs along the way as you ask them for directions because the reality is that they don't know where God is taking you, nor do they know the path that He has mapped out to get you there. Trust in the Lord with all of your heart and be determined not to lean to your own understanding (Prov. 3:5).

"Being confident of this very thing, that He which hath begun a good work in you will perform it until the day of Jesus Christ" (Phil. 1:6).

Moment of Reflection

You have all of the faith that you need. Place your faith in Jesus and allow Him to lead you where reason, logic, and your senses have worked to deter you.

His Name Shall Be Called

For unto us a child is born, unto us a Son is given: and the government shall be upon His shoulder: and His name shall be called Wonderful, Counselor, The mighty God, The everlasting Father, The Prince of Peace.

Isaiah 9:6

"His name shall be called Wonderful, Counselor, The mighty God, The everlasting Father, The Prince of Peace." Think about that for a moment. His name shall be called. Think of it this way: We can be introduced to a person and even get to know him or her on some level, but it will be the depth of that relationship that will dictate what adjectives we will be able to use when speaking of this person. After getting to know the person, we may be able to call him or her witty, patient, generous, kind, confidant, etc. However, the level of the relationship will dictate how many and how intimate the adjectives become, although these and many more attributes may reside in the individual. So it is with the Lord. He's all of those things that the Scriptures declare Him to be. It's up to each individual believer to establish a closeness with Him that will allow us to know as many facets of His character as possible.

Some only call Him Savior and will go no further than that in their knowledge of Him because they refuse to allow Him to be Lord in their lives. Yet He is Lord, and He is sovereign. He's a counselor, but we must be willing to hear Him and to follow His advice and leading as He prompts us through the Holy Ghost. He is a mighty God, and He is the Prince of Peace, but we won't know that if we feel that we, as children of the King, should be immune from trouble. There is a difference between the peace of God as promised in the Scriptures and the peace that the world gives, but we won't know that difference until we've encountered trouble, pain, and hardship that can't be eased naturally. The Lord has promised to give His peace even in the midst of bitter circumstances, and that's what makes His peace different from that which the world gives.

In the world, all must be calm in order for us to speak of having peace or being at peace. When we walk in the Spirit with the Prince of Peace, all can be in chaos around us, and He can speak peace to our souls in the midst of our storm. He gives us peace that passes our understanding. It's not that we deny the presence of the storm, the conflict, or the turmoil around us, but God gives an assurance in the heart of the believer that is truly beyond one's understanding. It's during these turbulent times that we realize that we've been supernaturally undergirded. There is no logical explanation for why we've not been overtaken by despair, fear, and terror, except that we are upheld by the powerful peace of God. He is our peace (Eph. 2:14).

God has promised to keep and to preserve His people through difficult times (see Ps. 121:5-8; 16:1; 41:2). At the appointed time, if we remain faithful, He will show Himself strong in and through our lives for His glory. God's property and possessions are solely His responsibility. He will not fail us! He will always prove to be "The mighty God" on our behalf.

While God shows His might through us in fighting battles and conquering our enemies, He also displays His wonderful mercy and willingness to forgive. He is a loving Father. The Scripture that has been referenced in Isaiah calls Him the "everlasting Father." "Everlasting" signifies having no beginning and no ending. Many have had to grow up without nurturing, loving fathers who were present and involved in their lives. But we can know our Savior and Lord in this way. We can call His name "everlasting Father"! For He is a Father who will forever love us, protect us, avenge us, provide for us, forgive us, and will impose righteous discipline in our lives for our benefit (Heb. 12:9-10). Unlike our natural fathers who corrected us for their own pleasure, we can trust Him as a Father who corrects and chastens His children for the purpose of our profit and that we may be partakers of His holiness. He alone has the ability and authority to cause all things to work together for our good.

As we allow Him to direct our paths, we can have an assurance that He will never lead us wrong. He desires to give us wise counsel. Anyone who has had a relationship with a counselor knows that a certain level of trust must be involved in that relationship in order for the counseling to be effective or to have a lasting affect. What a privilege to have the Lord of Lords, the King of Kings, and the Creator of all things as our Counselor! He will share great mysteries with us, and by His Spirit, He will lead us in our daily decisions. Jesus is the best coach, business partner, and advisor that one could ever have. The sad thing is that oftentimes believers take the position of not wanting to bother the Lord with "petty" things, or perhaps they feel that they don't need Him in their everyday decision-making. God's Word says to "acknowledge Him in all of your ways and He will direct your paths" (Prov. 3:6). All means all! It means even those things that we may feel are too small or insignificant to consult Him about. He can see where we can't, and He will direct our paths around pitfalls and snares that may not be evident to us. We have the opportunity to know Him as our Counselor, but far too many neglect this privilege, and thus are never able to testify of knowing the Savior in this way.

As we continue to grow in grace and in the knowledge of our Lord and Savior, Jesus Christ, we'll find ourselves assigning more and more adjectives to His name. We may be among those who call Him Deliverer, Healer, Teacher, Helper, Friend, Avenger, Lawyer, Advocate, and so much more! Our God is an awesome God, and He is more than Wonderful! The Scripture has told us what His name shall be called, but what do you call Him today?

Moment of Reflection

Think on your relationship with the Lord, and note all of the ways that you've come to know Him through your life experiences since being saved. Now ask Him to help you to know Him in new ways that will enhance your walk with Him and your impact on others.

The Power of the Exchange

And this He said to prove him: for He himself knew what
He would do.

John 6:6

Nothing that we possess is sufficient to carry out the tasks that
the Lord will place before us as our faith in Him is being
developed. In chapter 6 of the book of John, Jesus spoke to the
company of His disciples with regard to the multitude who had
followed Him to the other side of the Sea of Galilee. They followed
Him because of the miracles that they had seen Him perform. Philip
was singled out in order to be "proven" (v. 6). In what way was
he to be proven by such a situation? Philip's faith had to be tried,
but everyone who accompanied Jesus that day would soon learn the
power of the exchange.

The text indicates that there was a lesson to be learned and that
Jesus had the key to the solution, for verse 6 states that He (Jesus)
knew what He would do. The basis of this test was no different from
that which has been presented to men and women of God down
through the years. The Lord has always looked for those who are

willing to bring their insufficient means and to place them in His hands.

No matter how well we may know God's Word, most of us have a tendency to run to God and to present our problems from our own perspectives when we're faced with seemingly insurmountable challenges. Somehow in the thick of things, we tend to forget that He is with us and what His Word says about our situation.

Abram wondered how he would have an heir seeing that he had no seed and his wife was beyond childbearing years. Moses informed God of his stammering tongue and asked, "Who will listen to me?" Jeremiah shared with the Lord that he was "but a child." Each responded out of their place of insufficiency.

Let's consider what took place in the passage of Scripture found in John 6:5-12. The multitude had followed Jesus and His disciples, and the hour grew late without them having an opportunity to eat. They were hungry. The disciples found a boy in the midst of the crowd with two fish and five loaves of bread. Being a child, he was someone with no status and who had inadequate supply to meet the need. Yet he was willing to give the little that he had to the Lord's disciples, while he, along with others, must have realized that what he had wasn't enough. After taking notice of the little boy's lunch, which contained two small fish and five barley loaves, Andrew, Simon Peter's brother, asked, "But what are they among so many?"

Even people who walk closely with the Lord may sometimes try to place a value upon others or that which they contribute to the work of the Lord. What was brought to Jesus was irrelevant. Jesus needed His disciples to realize that His presence makes the difference in any situation. He is all-sufficient, all-knowing, and He will meet every need, not according to earthly means, but according to His riches in glory. If everyone present had brought a lunch and had decided to share, no doubt someone would still have gone away unsatisfied. There were children, women, and men in the midst, but the Bible tells us that after Jesus took the food, blessed it, and distributed it to His disciples, they served the multitude, and everyone was filled. Fragments were gathered after they had eaten. From little children to grown men, all appetites were satisfied because the Lord had made provision, and He always provides more than enough. Jesus already knew what He would do.

So then, how was Jesus to prove Philip? He asked Philip where they could buy bread so that the multitude could eat. Philip knew that they didn't have money to buy enough bread for everyone to get just a little. The Lord took this wonderful opportunity to teach that His presence always makes the difference. It is vital that we, too, recognize His presence and that we're willing to place what we have in His hands. We can trust Him for the outcome since we know that He makes provision for us.

Place what you have in the Lord's hands. He will bless it and return it to you in abundance so that needs can be met, provision can be made, and those around you who hunger will be filled.

Moment of Reflection

The Lord already knows what He will do in those situations that seem impossible to you. Just a simple exchange from your hand to His can make all the difference in the world, not just in your life, but in the lives of those around you.

The Faith Once Delivered

Beloved, when I gave all diligence to write unto you of the
common salvation, it was needful for me to write unto you,
and exhort you that ye should earnestly contend for the faith
which was once delivered unto the saints.

Jude 3

The anointing of God is not attached to one's position or title.
Higher elevation from man does not necessarily mean greater
anointing or power from God. The enemy's trick is to have believers
contending for positions, titles, and prestige in the church while
losing sight of the faith. Our enemy, the devil, seeks to keep us
distracted because if the church is ever infused with the faith once
delivered to the saints, we will have grasped something not only
worth fighting for but dying for.

The fire must begin to burn within the saints of God again. Jesus
gave a parable in Luke 18 with regard to the unjust judge who had no
fear of God or regard for man. Yet there was a woman who continued
to trouble him and to ask that he would avenge her of her adversary.
It was because of her persistence that the judge was persuaded to act

on her behalf. Jesus stated that we should take heed to this parable. He went on to say in Luke 18:7-8, "And shall not God avenge his own elect, which cry day and night unto Him, though He bear long with them? I tell you that He will avenge them speedily. Nevertheless when the Son of man cometh, shall He find faith on the earth?"

Great men and women of God have always been those who operated in and through faith, for without faith, it is impossible to please Him (Heb. 11:6). When we take the time to study and reflect on the faith that was once delivered to the saints and the price that they paid while contending for it, we are pushed beyond believing for houses, cars, spouses, and jobs. When Jesus asked if He would find faith on the earth when He returns, there is no doubt that the kind of faith that He will come for will have everything to do with things eternal.

The faith once delivered to the saints caused Noah to prepare an ark after being warned by God of things that had never been seen prior to that time. In the face of a rejecting and mocking society, he labored by faith. His family was saved, he condemned the world, and became heir of the righteousness which is by faith (Heb. 11:7). It was because of the faith once delivered to the saints that Abraham left his familiar homeland and went out into a far country that God had promised to him for an inheritance. This was the same faith that caused Sarah to receive strength to conceive seed and to deliver a child when she was past age. By this faith, Moses refused to be called the son of Pharaoh's daughter, although this could have made his life much easier. He chose rather to suffer affliction with the people of God than to enjoy the pleasures of sin for a season. It was the supernatural God of our faith who allowed these saints to see beyond the temporal and to be able to experience the benefits of trusting His ability to avenge, to deliver, and to empower them.

Their stories weren't glamorous, nor did they lead to stardom or recognition. However, they serve as examples and testimonies of victory for all believers who are willing to take hold of the faith that was delivered to them. The saints of old knew the secret. They knew that the more one is willing to give up, the more there is to gain. The higher that one desires to go in the things of God, the more abased we must be willing to become. When we surrender our wills, His will can be done in our lives, and it's better, always better. He is able to do exceeding abundantly above all that we could ever ask or think.

We must be determined to be full of God's Spirit and to seek Him for discernment, for we certainly will be faced with seducing spirits that have a form of godliness but deny His power. The faith once delivered to the saints requires that one must be born again, filled with the Spirit of God, and sanctified, or set apart, for service to Him alone. This faith gives us the power to minister to a dying world. Understand that as children of God, we will always be faced with opposing spirits that come to challenge our faith. God's standard hasn't changed. It is still faith in the shed blood of Jesus Christ, and that alone, that saves and empowers us for service in those things pertaining to the Kingdom of God. It is not left to each of us to find our own way. The Way has been made, and now by faith, we are challenged to walk in it.

Moment of Reflection

Let's dare to ask God to allow us to rise above that which our minds can grasp or perceive. That is where faith resides and comes alive in our lives. For with God nothing shall be impossible (Luke 1:37).

It's Not Your Dream!

And Joseph dreamed a dream, and he told it his brethren: and
they hated him yet the more.

Genesis 37:5

The enemy will always magnify what others are doing while
emphasizing what seems to be a place of "immobility" in our
lives. Despise not the day of small things. Don't give up, and don't
spend countless hours trying to network on your own. The Lord will
give opportunities and cause those relationships that are necessary
to the fulfillment of our destiny to surface in our lives. Things aren't
always as they appear! Those people whom we may have a tendency
to overlook and step around in order to get to someone of more
prominence may be the ones whom God has ordained to help get us
to the next level. He is the dream-giver, and only He knows what is
necessary to bring the dream to fruition in our lives!

Joseph was sold, locked up, forgotten about, lied to, lied on, and
somewhere through all of that, he must have wondered what would
become of the dream that God had given to him. Certainly, there

were times when he wondered if the dream was really from God (Gen. 37-41).

Through every trial and every struggle, Joseph experienced God's favor. It had nothing to do with him, but with the plan that God had put into place, which had to come to pass. After being betrayed by his brothers, being forgotten by the chief butler, who was released from prison, and being lied on by Potiphar's wife, Joseph had to come to the realization that God was for him and that He's more than the world against His people.

How foolish of Joseph's brothers to think that they could kill the dream by killing the dreamer! They thought that they could do away with the dream that Joseph had shared with them by simply ridding themselves of Joseph, by selling him, and therefore counting him out. But it wasn't his dream!

It's easy to see how Joseph was overly excited about the clear indication made through the dream that he would be someone great among his brothers, and he wanted to share this excitement with his family. However, God had to change his perception and help him to grasp another perspective on the interpretation of the dream. God had to move him from the place where his heart cried out, "Lord, show my brothers who I am!" to a place wherein he was willing to say, "Lord, it's not about me; now I yield and ask that You show my brothers who You arc through me." There's a difference! It's evident that Joseph realized this difference in perspective as we read his response to his brothers at the time of their reconciliation in Genesis 50:20: "But as for you, ye thought evil against me; but God meant it unto good, to bring to pass, as it is this day, to save much people alive." Some of us keep trying to prove to others that God has called us and that His hand is upon us. Whatever task God has placed within us to be accomplished, rest assured that He will work it out down to the minutest detail. Every step of the way, the Spirit of God will constantly remind us that it's not about us. God will continue to chip away at us and "our stuff" until it's no longer "us," but Christ who lives in us whom others see and experience. No matter what level we may be blessed to attain in the things of God, people don't need an experience with us; they need an experience with the true and living God!

Unless we're willing to allow the Lord to lead us through places of great opposition and trial, we'll just be reciting empty words when we declare, "If God be for us, He's more than the world against us!" (Rom. 8:31b). Just as Joseph experienced testing on the road to his destiny, we, too, must go through times of testing. It's through these times that God is glorified in and through our lives, as He teaches us with each test to trust Him and to give Him praise. Our tests come to build us, not to destroy us, so we can expect victory and deliverance each time. We must view times of opposition and trial as opportunities to learn more about the character of our Lord and His love for us. Through them we find the means to see His hand move in our lives and in the lives of those around us. It had to have been devastating for Joseph to learn that after sharing his ministry gift of interpretation of dreams with the Pharaoh's butler and baker, with whom he had been imprisoned, he was forgotten by the chief butler after the butler was released (Gen. 40:23). But God's plan for him was the pit, the prison, and then the palace.

From the very beginning when Joseph was betrayed by his brothers and was in a pit looking at dirt walls, God was setting the stage before him. God had gone before him preparing favor in the king's heart and preparing a place for him in the king's palace. This certainly wasn't obvious to Joseph during his time of great testing and opposition. Since we have the privilege of knowing the end of Joseph's story, it can be a source of encouragement to those of us who have such a great desire for God's will to be done in our lives. During the times when it seems as though everything is working in opposition to the dream that the Lord has placed within our spirits, we must remember Joseph's story. God's favor went before him, and as He leads us in the pathway of our ordained destiny, His favor precedes us as well. He works out the plans for each stage of our lives before we get there. Just know that where you sit now is not your final destination, but God is working things out in your tomorrows. Favor awaits you; the favor of God rests upon you, and your place of destiny is sure! It was established before the foundation of the world!

Our heavenly Father is the dream-giver. He gives dreams and places desires within our hearts, which lead us to our destiny in Him. The vision, or dream, that God gives is always greater than our ability to bring it to pass. He will set up circumstances, relationships, and opportunities that otherwise never would have come our way, if we'll yield ourselves to His plan and His purpose for our lives.

Proverbs 18:16 reads, "A man's gift maketh room for him, and bringeth him before great men." This certainly happened in the life of Joseph. Although he had been forgotten by the chief butler, the need in the Pharaoh's life to have his own troubling dream interpreted (Gen. 41:8) caused the circumstance wherein his life was divinely connected with the life of Joseph. Consequently, the lives of all the Egyptians and those of Joseph's kindred would be forever changed. Those who seemed to be "key" people in Joseph's life all along the way had forgotten him, but it would be God who ultimately remembered him and brought him to his place of destiny before great men.

No doubt, Joseph came to realize that he only dreamed the dream but that it wasn't his. It had come from the One who always does exceeding abundantly above all that we're able to ask or think. Our God is the dream-giver! He has set in motion that which is necessary for each of His children to succeed in our walk with Him. We must give back to Him that which He has entrusted to us — our gifts, talents, aspirations, and dreams — in order for Him to bring to pass the greatest good for our lives. Remember, it's not your dream!

Moment of Reflection

Refuse to seek the approval of others before being willing to obey God. Remember that only God knows exactly where He's taking you, and He alone is able to get you there.

ENCOURAGEMENT FOR MY SISTERS

G ood morning, Esther; you're beautiful! Oh, I know that isn't your real name, for some of you have chosen to hide your true identity for fear of rejection. Others of you have played your "role" for so long until you have no idea who you truly are or what your purpose is. Finally, I must tell you that some of you have been purposefully hidden and kept a secret until such a time as this.

Many souls are tied to your destiny. Your true identity must first be revealed before the miracle of your deliverance and the deliverance of those who are connected to you can be manifested.

There is no need for competition. You have already been chosen. The King's scepter is extended to you. You, along with your assignment, shall live. What a time of favor! He set this time aside for you even before the foundation of the world so that you could come into His presence and make your petitions known.

As we stand in the outer court, there is a sense of urgency in our spirits as the King summons us to be ushered into His presence . . . into the very inner courts. . . .

Now, dare to make your requests known unto Him! He waits to hear from you!

Leslie

SENTIMENTS OF MY HEART

There is no ministry except it comes from God. We must guard against just becoming a part of "church systems," wherein we begin to aspire after titles and positions after we've come to know Christ.

Our aspirations must be for greater things in God and not necessarily greater or loftier positions within the church. When a closer walk with the Lord becomes our focus, we're not envious of others as though they have the power or means to keep us from anything that the Lord might have for us. We are assured that promotion comes from the Lord and Him alone. What are you aspiring to and why? Whose dream are you chasing?

The reality is that there is so much within me that I long for! My desires run deep, and my dreams far surpass all that I've seen or know at this present time in my life. Surely, if others were able to see the visions that I have, they would look at me and say, "Huh? No, surely not her!" But I know that there's more in me, there's more for me! I just need to have Your strength and guidance, Lord, in order to attain and obtain it.

What *would* I do if I just wasn't afraid? What *could* I do if I just wasn't afraid?

If only I wasn't held captive by the self that I've been until now. But isn't that why You came—to set the captives free? Even if that means freedom from ourselves and the prisons of our minds and the comfort of "small thinking."

I know that there's more; I want more, and I need more! Lord, I come now to empty myself before You. Every heartfelt desire I now lay at Your feet. My soul is tired of striving, and my eyes grow weary from trying to see my way. My mind becomes more and more baffled as I attempt to figure things out. I pray for Your peace. Impart vision unto me and the guidance of Your Holy Spirit so that I may know the path that I must take. Finally, grant me the faith to trust You when the direction that my life takes makes no logical sense to me. You are my Lord, my Guide, my Protector, my Provider, and my Friend. Oh, how I love You!

As I constantly seek to know who I am, one assurance remains, and that is the assurance that I am Yours and that my true identity lies within the confines of Your will for my life. Thank You, faithful Father. Thank You, Jesus, my faithful Friend. Thank You, Holy Spirit, my faithful Companion and Guide!

Forever yours,

Leslie

Printed in the United States
201430BV00002B/1-261/A